LARGE PRINT

READ ALOUD
CLASSIC TALES

Foolish Brahmin and his Goat
and other stories...

Retold by
VANEETA VAID

Nita Mehta
Publications
Enriching Young Minds

LARGE PRINT

READ ALOUD TALES
CLASSIC TALES

Foolish Brahmin and His Goat
and other stories...

Nita Mehta Publications

Corporate Office
3A/3, Asaf Ali Road, New Delhi 110 002
Phone: +91 11 2325 2948, 2325 0091
Telefax: +91 11 2325 0091
E-mail: nitamehta@nitamehta.com
Website: www.nitamehta.com

First Print 2014

Printed in India at Infinity Advertising Services (P) Ltd, New Delhi

Editorial and Marketing office
E-159, Greater Kailash II, New Delhi 110 048

Cover Designed by: flyingtrees

Typesetting by National Information Technology Academy
3A/3, Asaf Ali Road, New Delhi 110 002

Distributed by :
NITA MEHTA BOOKS
3A/3, Asaf Ali Road, New Delhi - 02

Distribution Centre :
D16/1, Okhla Industrial Area, Phase-I,
New Delhi - 110020
Tel.: 26813199, 26813200
E-mail: nitamehta.mehta@gmail.com

Contributing Writers:
Subhash Mehta
Tanya Mehta

Editorial & Proofreading:
Rajesh
Ramesh

Price: Rs. 145/-   US $ 6.95   UK £ 3.95

CONTENTS

INTRODUCTION

This book is a collection of short stories from the Indian classics. There are stories of wit, humour, love, betrayal, pride and courage, explained in a simple and interesting manner.

Every story is complemented with beautiful illustrations which fascinate children. It is hoped that the book will not only entertain children but also inculcate in them good values and worldly wisdom.

TRUE FRIENDS

In a forest, there lived a brown mouse, a black crow, a deer and a tortoise. They were best friends.

One day, they met at the lake. However, the deer was missing.

"The deer is never late," said the mouse. "He runs very fast! What could have happened today?"

"Perhaps, he is in some DANGER," said the crow.

"I will fly over the forest and see if I can find him," said the crow. Up soared the crow!

Oh dear! He saw the deer below, **trapped** in a net. He informed the others. They rushed to the deer, except the tortoise of course!

"The mouse can gnaw the net and rescue our friend." It was decided.

The mouse immediately started biting the net with his sharp teeth. Soon the deer was free. By then, the tortoise had also reached there, CRAWLING slowly all the way.

Suddenly, the Hunter returned. The friends hid. The Tortoise, however, was not so quick!

The hunter realized that the deer had escaped.

"Oh, what bad luck. Now what will I have for dinner?" said the hunter. Just then he saw the tortoise crawling towards the bush.

"**HA, HA**, you will be my dinner," said the hunter. He dropped the tortoise in his bag and started walking home.

The crow, above saw this! He called out to his friends, "Our friend, the tortoise is in danger!"

"I have a plan," said the deer.

The hunter walking home, suddenly saw the deer grazing in front of him.

"A deer? what luck!" said the hunter.

The hunter dropped the bag. He ran after the deer to **CATCH** him.

That is when the mouse immediately cut open the bag with his teeth. The tortoise *slipped* out of the bag. He hid under a bush.

The Hunter, of course, could not catch the deer. On his return, he saw the tortoise had escaped too!

"I am very **unlucky**," the hunter said sadly. "First the deer got away! Now even this slow tortoise has escaped. I will have to sleep hungry tonight!"

The tortoise, the mouse, the crow and the deer smiled as they quietly watched the hunter leave.

THE UNCOOKED RICE

Akbar, the emperor of India, was a **GREAT** ruler.

Birbal was Akbar's favourite courtier. That made everyone in the court *jealous*. The other courtiers were always plotting against Birbal.

Once, at a *court discussion,* Akbar said, "Once a wise man said that people will do anything for money.

But I believe that there are certain things that nobody will do, even if I were to offer a **GREAT REWARD**. There is a lake opposite the palace gardens. No one would *dare* to stand in that ice cold water for a whole night, with nothing to warm himself, even if I would offer a great reward for doing so."

Everyone in the court agreed with what Akbar said, except Birbal.

"I wish I could **agree** with you, your majesty," Birbal said, "but, I will find a man who can stand in the lake and win the reward."

"If you find such a man I will give him a thousand **gold coins**," declared Akbar.

The next day, Birbal brought a WOODCUTTER to Akbar's court. The Woodcutter was willing to stand in the lake to win the reward.

The woodcutter stepped into the ice cold water of the lake. The whole night the woodcutter stood in the cold water shaking **FIERCELY**. At sunrise, he stepped out of the water.

"I have done it!" exclaimed the woodcutter.

Akbar, though surprised, called for the reward.

As Akbar called for the coins, another courtier, Abdul Rahman, saw this as an **opportunity** to impress the emperor and be one up on Birbal.

"And what were you doing when you were in the freezing water?" **questioned** Abdul Rahman.

"I looked at the palace lights **glowing** in the dark," answered the woodcutter.

"Then, you **cheated**," said Abdul Rahman. "The reward was for the person who would spend the night without having anything to warm himself. You derived warmth from the palace lights. Thus, you don't deserve the reward."

Akbar agreed with what Abdul Rahman said and the poor woodcutter was not given the reward. The woodcutter sadly went home.

The next day, Birbal invited Akbar and Abdul Rahman for dinner to his house. Akbar and Abdul Rahman waited for a long time, but no dinner was served. "Sorry for the delay, your majesty. But the rice is taking a long time to cook," Birbal said **politely**.

"It is only a little rice. Why is it taking so long to cook?" asked Akbar, getting irritated.

Birbal took his guests to a **COURTYARD** where a pot was tied to a high tree branch. Underneath the pot, a small fire was burning on the ground.

"What is this **STUPIDITY**?" asked Abdul Rahman, "This rice can never be cooked. How can the heat of this fire reach the pot so far away?"

"It is not that far," Birbal replied politely. "If the woodcutter can be warmed by looking at the palace lights a mile away, then this rice can surely be cooked with the heat of the fire, which is closer to the rice."

"I have learnt my lesson, Birbal," Akbar said smiling. "Tomorrow morning, the woodcutter will be given his reward twice over."

CROWS AND THE SNAKE

A family of crows LIVED in a tree. One day, a large snake made its home in a hole in the same tree. Mama and Papa crow were very **worried**. They knew the snake could eat their babies.

But they could not stop the snake from living there. What they *feared* happened soon. Their babies went missing. They knew the snake had eaten them. The next time, when the mama crow laid eggs, papa crow said,

"We should be *careful* this time."

One day, when the father crow had gone out to get food, the snake once again ate the babies. Mama crow could do nothing.

"We need help. We will go and meet our friend, the fox. He is clever. He will help us," decided papa crow.

The crows went to the fox and *told* him what had happened.

The fox thought for a while and then said,

"Alright! Here is the plan. Tomorrow morning the ladies of the king's palace will go to the river for their bath. They will remove their ornaments and clothes and keep it on the river bank before entering the water. Their servants will be standing at a distance keeping a watch on the valuables. When nobody is near, one of you pick up a necklace and fly away. Make a lot of noise as you are flying so that the servants see you. They will run after you to get the *necklace* back. You fly straight to your tree and drop the necklace into the snake's hole."

The crows **agreed** to follow the fox's plan. The next morning they went to the river. As soon as the ladies kept their ornaments and clothes on the *river bank* and entered the water, the mother crow picked up a necklace and flew away.

The servants followed the crows and saw the mother crow dropping the necklace into the snake's hole.

"Let us use a long stick to take out the necklace from the hole," one of the *servants* said. When the stick was put inside the hole, the snake felt **disturbed** and came out hissing. The servants saw the snake. After killing it, they took out the necklace from the hole. The crows were happy that the snake was dead.

FOOLISH BRAHMIN AND HIS GOAT

One day a Brahmin received a goat as a gift from a friend. Three thieves saw the Brahmin **CARRYING** the goat. They decided to steal it.

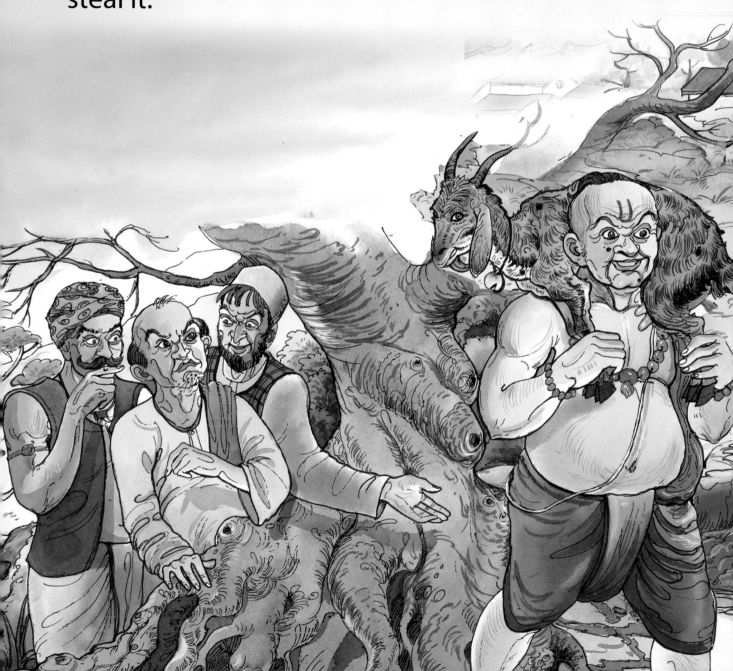

One of the **THIEVES** walked up to the Brahmin and said, "Holy Brahmin, why are you carrying a dog on your shoulders?"

"Are you blind? I am carrying a goat!" **exclaimed** the Brahmin.

Shrugging, the thief went away.

The Brahmin continued walking. The second thief came up to him. He looked at the Brahmin and the goat and said, "Sir, why are you carrying a dead calf on your shoulders?"

"This is a live goat. I have just received this as a gift from my friend."

This thief also shrugged and went away.

Now the Brahmin was worried. 'I wonder why those two men said that?' thought the Brahmin.

Soon, he met the third thief. "A Brahmin should never carry a donkey. In fact you should not even TOUCH such an animal," said the third thief.

The Brahmin was very *confused*. This was the third man he had met. And each of them had seen the goat as something else. The first one saw it as a dog, the second as a dead calf and the third as a donkey.

'Is this goat a **monster** or a *demon* that can change into something else every few minutes?' the Brahmin thought to himself. 'Perhaps, these men were telling the *truth*.'

The Brahmin was so frightened that he immediately threw the goat down. Then he ran home as fast as he could.

The third thief picked up the goat and *hurried* back to his friends. The thieves were happy as their plan was **successful**.

THE MONKEY'S ADVICE

Once upon a time, there lived a king who had many monkeys. He kept these **monkeys** to entertain his son.

Besides the monkeys, a herd of sheep was also kept at the palace grounds. One of the sheep was always running into the royal kitchen to nibble at whatever he could find. A wise, old monkey had **WATCHED** this happen many times. He called all the monkeys and said to them, "This sheep is going to get us all killed one day. The cooks become very angry when the sheep enters the kitchen. **Suppose**, one day, they throw a lighted wood at the sheep. Then, the sheep's thick wool will catch fire. To save himself, the sheep will run into the **stables** near the kitchen.

When the sheep rolls on the hay to put off the fire, the hay will catch fire and burn the whole stable. The horses will get burnt and the doctors would say that the best cure for burns of horses is monkey fat. Then, the king will order to kill all the monkeys to provide that fat. Let us get out of here before we are all killed."

The other monkeys ignored the advice of the wise monkey and laughed at him.

The old monkey became sad on hearing this. All the same, the old monkey left the palace.

After a few days, the sheep again ran into the royal kitchen. This time, one of the cooks threw a lighted wood at the sheep.

When his wool caught fire, the sheep ran into the stables, where the hay caught fire. Soon, the whole stable was **BURNING**. In this fire, many horses were severely burnt.

When the king received the news, he was very sad. He called all the doctors for their **advice**. The doctors said, "Applying monkey fat to the burnt areas will **RELIEVE** the pain."

Immediately, the king ordered that all the monkeys be killed and their fat **collected**. One by one, all the monkeys were **killed**.

REVENGE OF THE MONKEY

The old, wise monkey heard the sad news of his friends' death as per the king's order. He wanted to take REVENGE and teach the king a lesson. In his wanderings, one day, he sat by a river thinking. Suddenly, he noticed *footsteps* leading into the river; but none coming out!

'Surely, there lives a **beast** in the river who eats anyone who enters the lake,' the monkey thought.

So, the monkey took a lotus stalk, **dipped** it into the river and SUCKED water through it.

Just then, a **vicious** looking beast came out from the middle of the river.

"You are a very CLEVER monkey," said the beast. "I eat anyone who enters the river. What can I do for you?"

"How many men can you eat at a time?" asked the monkey.

"I can eat several thousands! However, only if they are in the water. I have no STRENGTH on land," answered the beast.

The beast was wearing a beautiful diamond necklace around his neck. The monkey saw it and said, "I have a plan. Lend me your necklace."

The beast gave the necklace to the monkey. Wearing it around his neck, the monkey went to the king's palace. When the king's soldiers saw the monkey wearing the necklace, they were amazed. They took the monkey to their king.

From where did you get that necklace?" questioned the king.

"O king," said the monkey, "not far from here, there is a river. If anyone enters it, he comes out wearing a diamond necklace."

"I *believe* you," said the king. "I will lead my ARMY to the river and then I will have thousands of diamond necklaces."

"Show us that river," the king ordered the monkey.

As soon as they *reached* the river, the king's soldiers dived into the river.

'My soldiers will soon be back with the necklaces,' thought the greedy king. The king waited for a long time but none of his soldiers came out of the river.

"Why are the soldiers taking so much time?"

The king asked the monkey.

The monkey quickly climbed up the branch of a tall tree and replied,

"Foolish king, you have been blinded by greed. Your soldiers will never RETURN as they have been eaten up by a beast who lives in the river. When you killed my friends, I had vowed to take revenge. Now all your soldiers are dead. I spared you because you are a king."

THE JUDGE

A partridge **lived** in her nest under a large banyan tree. She had been living there for many years.

One day, the partridge left her nest to **search** for food.

Meanwhile, a rabbit saw the partridge's empty nest. "Nobody lives here, I will make it my house."

So, the rabbit started living in the partridge's nest. After a few days, the patridge returned home. When she saw the rabbit in her nest, she was very angry.

"What are you doing here?" the partridge said **angrily**. "This is my house."

"Your house," SHOUTED the rabbit. "I found this house empty. Nobody was living here. It is my house now. I have been living here for many days."

The quarrel between the rabbit and the partridge went for a long time. Many animals and birds gathered around them and listened to their **ARGUMENTS**. But nobody could say to whom the house belonged.

One of the animals said,

"Why don't you find someone who can be the judge. Take your dispute to him and let him decide to whom the house belongs."

The rabbit and the partridge saw a cat. The cat saw them too and immediately, he held up a string of prayer beads, closed his eyes and prayed at the top of his voice. Though the rabbit and the partridge knew that the cat was their natural enemy; but seeing him pray, they decided to trust him.

After a few minutes, the cat opened his eyes.

47

"O holy cat," said the partridge, "a little argument has arisen between this rabbit and me. Please listen to our dispute and decide who is right. We make you the judge. You may punish whoever you find is in the wrong."

The patridge and the rabbit babbled their complaints.

The cat was **silent** for a few moments. Then he said, "I am old now and cannot see or hear well. I have not understood your case. Come closer and tell me all over again."

The partridge and the rabbit were no longer afraid of the cat. They trusted him and moved closer to him. As soon as they came close, the cat pounced on them and killed them.

48